Ten Days to Justice

Justice

(Richard is Missing)

Ten Days to Justice

(Richard is Missing)

A True Account of a Kidnap-Murder on the Texas-Mexico Border

Dennis W. Harlan

ELEVATION PRESS
OF COLORADO

Ten Days to Justice
(Richard is Missing)

A True Account of a Kidnap-Murder
on the Texas-Mexico Border

by Dennis W. Harlan

Copyright © 2009 by Dennis Harlan

Originally published in 2009 under the title *Richard is Missing* and the now out-of-print ISBN 978-1-4392-5821-7 by Mercury HeartLink Press, Silver City, New Mexico, who have given permission to publish this new edition.

Cover and interior design and interior formatting by Donna Marie Benjamin of Elevation Press of Colorado.

Photo credits:
Handcuffs sitting on U.S. and Mexico flags—Photo 312141295 | Border Patrol © Jj Gouin | Dreamstime.com
Handcuffs (alone)—Photo 183406465 © Ruzanna Arutyunyan | Dreamstime.com

Dennis W. Harlan
17532 Surface Creek Road
Cedaredge, CO 81413

Ordering information: Quantity sales. Special discounts are available on quantity purchases by book clubs, corporations, associations, and others. For details, contact the publisher at the address above.

ISBN 978-0-932624-27-7

Second printing, 2024

1. Main category— [True Crime] 2. Other categories— [Police Procedures]

ELEVATION PRESS
OF COLORADO

Cedaredge, Colorado
www.elevation-press-books.com

for Richard

Contents

Acknowledgements

Inspiration to write this book came first from my loving family: my wife, Valerie, and daughter, Erin, and son, Justin. I also drew inspiration from favorite authors: James Kuykendall, *O Plata O Plomo* (*Silver or Lead*), Joaquin Jackson, *One Ranger* and *One Ranger Returns*, and Dorothy Swartz writing as Dot Ryan, *Corrigans' Pool*. In addition, Professor Eva Brown, Adams State College, who first proofread the first draft of the manuscript and made me believe a retired Customs Agent with a few years of college could actually write a book!

I would also like to recognize Lori Kester, a senior English major at Adams State for editing my "Ingress" (chuckle). I also include my friends and colleagues of Special Agents of the U.S. Customs Service who watched my back during ongoing investigations and the "ups and downs" of my career.

Thanks also to Pamela Warren Williams and her late husband Stewart Warren of New Mexico's Mercury Heartlink Press who first published this book in 2009. Ms. Williams has graciously given her blessing for me to move forward with republication.

Finally, I'm very grateful for the work of Don and Donna Marie Benjamin of Elevation Press of Colorado, an independent publishing house located in Cedaredge. This dynamic couple designed and reformatted my out-of-print book and shepherded it through the re-publishing process.

Dedication

This book is dedicated to Richard Mack Latham and the men and women who hold the line and protect our way of life and freedom.

Proceeds over and above expenses will be donated to The Tunnel to Towers Foundation. The mission of The Tunnel to Towers Foundation is to honor the sacrifice of firefighter Stephen Siller who laid down his life to save others on September 11, 2001. The Foundation also honors military and first responders who continue to make the supreme sacrifice of life and limb for our country. The Foundation is recognized as a tax-exempt 501(c)(3) non-profit organization. Contributions are tax-deductible.

Direct donations can be made at the Foundation website (https://t2t.org/). Or by telephone using a credit card, or through the mail:

The Tunnel to Towers Foundation
2361 Hylan Blvd.
Staten Island, NY 10306
(718) 987-1931

Prologue

Going the "extra mile" to see that justice is done

Prologue

From August, 1978 to April, 1985 I was the Resident Agent for the U.S. Customs Service Office of Investigations in Del Rio, Texas. At that time, we were the investigative arm of the Customs Service, handling investigations and presenting for prosecution a variety of cases involving smuggling, fraud, money laundering, illegal exports, and internal investigations.

The date was January 27, 1984, a Friday evening, and I had not been home from work more than fifteen minutes when the telephone rang. It was Ralph Sinclair, Supervisory Customs Inspector at the International Port of Entry (IPOE) at Del Rio, Texas. Ralph said that I'd better get down to the port—Richard was missing. Ralph explained there had been an armed robbery of a jewelry store in Acuña, Mexico and he suspected Richard may have been kidnapped by the perpetrators. Richard Latham, a U.S. Customs Inspector, was last seen in the Secondary Inspection area at the port during the robbery alert and was nowhere to be found.

The Inspectors rotate positions during their tour of duty, moving from Primary to Secondary; to the cargo dock and then inside the office, depending on their assignment that day. They also take rest and lunch breaks on the premises but it is rare for them to leave the Port of Entry complex, especially without the permission of a supervisor. Ciudad Acuña, Coahuila, Mexico is located just across the Rio Grande River which forms the international border between Mexico and the United States.

Richard Mack Latham, 50 years of age, had been a Customs Inspector for approximately

10 years and had been a Customs Patrol Officer before that. Richard was raised on a ranch near Pandale, Texas; he was divorced and had two daughters. His brother, Pete, was at that time a Mounted Inspector or "Tick Rider" for the U.S. Department of Agriculture in Del Rio and is now deceased. Another brother, Bobby, was a U.S. Border Patrolman in Brackettville, Texas, and is now retired in Del Rio. Richard had the reputation of being a good, dependable officer and was known for his wry, dry West Texas humor and barnyard philosophy. Most everybody liked Richard and I considered him a personal friend. About a week before, Richard and I had been sitting in a local "gin-mill" commiserating the state of the Customs Service and the world in general. I remember one of Richard's favorite sayings. Whenever he'd be asked to do something extra, he'd always say, "It's no step for a stepper" and then he would do it.

I proceeded to the port, about a ten-minute drive from my residence, and on the way I contacted Sector, our communications center in Houston, to notify Special Agents Robert Sam Hale and Don Mog, who were assigned to the Del Rio Office, of the situation. Don came on the air immediately and, after some discussion of the situation, advised he would contact the local office of the Texas Department of Public Safety and coordinate the highway search. Sam Hale was on the air shortly, and agreed to meet me at the port.

We met with Jack Alsup, Port Director, and Ralph Sinclair, Customs Supervisor, at the Port and were briefed on the following facts. At approximately 4:00 p.m., the Port of Entry (POE) was advised by Mexican Authorities that an armed robbery of a jewelry store had occurred in Ciudad Acuña. The initial information was that the suspects were driving a light colored Toyota sedan and the POE was placed on alert. The focus of all port personnel was to look for that vehicle and, shortly thereafter, it was discovered that Richard was missing. A search of the immediate port area, telephone calls to Richard's home, friends, and relatives met with negative results.

The word of Richard's disappearance was spread and local law enforcement officials began arriving at the port. Jack Richardson, U.S. Border Patrol Deputy Chief and Sergeant Lee Smith, Texas Department of Public Safety (DPS), advised that they would quickly establish highway checkpoints and land and air search grids, and coordinate those efforts. The Border Patrol usually has a number of aircraft operating in the area which would facilitate immediate coverage of the area.

A check of the Treasury Enforcement Computer System (TECS) and interviews with port personnel disclosed that Richard was last seen at the Secondary Search Area of the port inspecting a white 1975 Pontiac Gran Prix bearing Texas license plate VLS 318 around the time the port alert was initiated. TECS is a computer generated lookout system employed by the Customs Service to place lookouts for suspects and violators by name and license number. The system also includes other applications but for the purpose of this book, those applications have no bearing and much of the system and its use are classified. The Gran Prix was found to be registered to a party in El Paso who had recently sold the vehicle to Ricardo Velasquez, who had not re-registered the car. Follow up investigation identified Velazquez and his residence in El Paso. A subsequent interview of his mother by FBI agent Charles Riley determined Velasquez had been out of town for three or four days but still had the car.

At that time, Del Rio, Texas, was a city of approximately 30,000 people located about 150 miles southwest of San Antonio on the Mexican border. It is the home of Laughlin Air Force Base (AFB), one of the busiest pilot training bases in the United States Air Force, and was the site of U-2 Flights over Cuba during the "Cuban Missile Crisis." Del Rio is also the burial spot of Judge Roy Bean, "Law West of the Pecos" at the Whitehead Museum.

For many years, many people recognized Del Rio, Texas, and Ciudad Acuña, Coahuila, Mexico with the radio station XERF and "Wolfman Jack" who used to play "Rock & Roll" music of the 50s and 60s and encourage listeners to send in money for "an autographed picture of Jesus Christ." The 250,000 kilowatt XERF transmitter was located in Mexico and boomed this unique message and music all over the U.S. and Canada. The radio station was founded by Dr. John R. Brinkley, who was not a licensed doctor but had experimented with xenotransplantation of goat glands in humans as a means of curing male impotence, and was an advertising and radio pioneer who began the era of Mexican border blasters.

Del Rio, Texas, is also the site and location utilized by one of my favorite radio and television talk show hosts, Don Imus, in his book *God's Other Son*.

According to a Chamber of Commerce article on the Internet, Del Rio lies on the northwestern edges of the Tamaulipan Thorn-scrub, also called the South Texas brush country. It is also near the southwestern corner of the Edwards Plateau which is on the western fringe of the famous oak savanna-covered Texas Hill Country that is dotted with numerous small springs. One of these is the San Felipe Springs which provides a constant flow of water to San Felipe Creek. The creek supplied fresh water for drinking and irrigation to early settlers of Del Rio and is still the town's water supply. It has been estimated the water flow is approximately 19 second-feet or about 12 million gallons a day.

West of Del Rio to about the Pecos River, there is a mix of desert shrub and steppe vegetation, depending on the soil type where the gray-leafed Ceniza or purple sage and acacia and grama grasses are dominant flora members of the local landscape. The terrain is mostly level but some areas are dissected with substantial canyons and drainages, though none of the upland areas are high or large enough to be considered mountains.

The climate is semi-arid in moisture and subtropical in temperature. Humidity is more often high than low, with periodic morning fog due to the Gulf of Mexico air masses moving northwest into the area. This gives Del Rio and adjacent areas the effect of being in a coastal dry land area, even though the Gulf of Mexico is over 300 miles away. Such humid periods alternate with periods of hot and dry desert air masses in the spring and fall, or cold and dry Great Plains air masses during winter months. Moisture rarely lasts long enough for weather systems to react with it to create much precipitation.

Summers are long, hot, and frequently humid. Winter months vary between sunny, warm, cloudy, and cool weather, depending on the wind direction and jet stream location. Snow or freezing rain is rare, and such wintry precipitation does not occur most winters, or last long enough to be of consequence except when a "Blue Norther" blows in. A "Blue Norther" is an arctic cold blast that can send temperatures plummeting. There is nothing of geological significance between Del Rio and the Arctic Circle other than a three strand barbed wire fence.

As of the census of 2000, there were about 30,000 residents in Del Rio. The racial make-up of the city was about 80 percent Hispanic or Latino and eight percent white.

Del Rio sits on beautiful Lake Amistad. "Amistad" means "friendship" in Spanish, and when full, the lake contains about 17 thousand surface acre-feet of water. The Rio Grande River was dammed during the 1950s by the construction of Amistad Dam for flood control and irrigation further down the Rio Grand Valley. Water from the Pecos, Devil, and Concho rivers flow into the Rio Grande water system.

Those of us that are, or have been, involved in law enforcement, understand the problems of jurisdiction. City police seem to be at odds with the local sheriff's department, and they all seem to be at odds with state officials at times and everybody can resent the federal government and its agencies. Federal agencies all have primary jurisdiction in some areas but sometimes jurisdiction seems to overlap. On the evening of this incident, I was informed by Assistant U.S. Attorney, Dan Maeso of San Antonio, that the Federal Bureau of Investigation (FBI), San Antonio, was sending some 40 agents to Del Rio and they thought they would be in charge of the investigation.

Many federal agencies do not have investigative branches and the FBI assumes assault investigations for those agencies. As it turns out, back in the Hoover days, there was a White Paper (inter-agency agreement) executed between the Justice and Treasury Departments that basically stated that when one of ours, a U.S. Customs Officer or Agent, was assaulted or killed, the Customs Office of Investigation would handle the investigation. It took a while for this situation to resolve itself. FBI Group Supervisor, Joe Gannon, San Antonio, who had been a policeman in Brownsville, Texas, was a stabilizing factor during this "turf battle" and eventually this matter was resolved with us being the primary agency. The only thing I was concerned about was finding Richard.

There ensued a major law enforcement search for Richard. The Del Rio Fire Department and volunteers searched many of the roads and bar ditches in and around Del Rio.

The next day, January 28, Richard's body was found by woodcutters in a ditch alongside Highway 277, upriver from Eagle Pass, Texas, and east of Del Rio, brutally murdered. Richard's hands were handcuffed behind his back and he had received two bullet wounds to his back.

Almost simultaneously, two of the perpetrators of the crime, Rafael Calderon and Jesus Ramirez, were encountered by Texas DPS Troopers near Dryden, Texas, west of Del Rio on Highway 90 West. Ramirez had apparently accidentally killed himself by gunshot during the apprehension. The jewelry taken in the armed robbery in Acuña was recovered from

Calderon and on the body of Ramirez. Documentary evidence found at that scene and recovered from Mexico led to the identity of the other two perpetrators, Ricardo Velasquez and Samuel Olguin, who were subsequently arrested in El Paso, all within ten days time.

Considering the nature of the crime, and the remoteness of this vast area of West Texas, it is amazing that Richard's body was found and the persons responsible for the crime were apprehended in such a short time. I can only attribute this to outstanding law enforcement action and to the dedication and cooperation of those agencies participating. Those of us in law enforcement always try hard to solve crimes but when one of our own is taken and brutally murdered, we all seem to go the "extra mile" to see that justice is done. We had some "luck" in that Richard's body was found and two of the violators were apprehended a day after the incident at the International Bridge but by going full boat, twenty-four hours a day and never giving up, we made our own luck.

I am telling this story as the agent in charge of the investigation and I am sharing the results of a quickly put together task force of local, county, state, and federal authorities which investigated the crime, wrote the Criminal Case Report, and prepared the case for federal and state prosecution. Included are the results of interviews of witnesses and the defendants arrested for the crime, recovery of physical and documentary evidence and assistance by the following key investigators in this matter: William W. Barnes, IV, Investigator, Val Verde County District Attorney's Office; John Martin, Detective, Del Rio Police Department; and Don E. Weathermon, Special Agent, Federal Bureau of Investigation, San Antonio, Texas.

Our investigative team was greatly assisted and directed by Thomas Franklin Lee, District Attorney for Val Verde County and Assistant U.S. Attorney Daniel Maeso, San Antonio, Texas. The following story about this crime and the subsequent investigation is offered as it happened. Facts of this case are taken from the Criminal Case Report, prepared by the above named investigators and myself. Three of the four perpetrators were captured; one shot himself while officers were attempting to apprehend him and two of the assailants, who became cooperating defendants, gave sworn statements against the shooter, Calderon. The perpetrators were all brought to justice in just 10 days!

Customs Agents are not routinely trained in homicide investigation unless they have previous experience with a police or sheriff's department. In this instance, I had no training, but thanks to the experience of Detective Martin and Investigator Barnes, who had a lot of homicide experience, they basically led me through that portion of the case. Investigation is investigation but homicide is unique. You only get one chance at the crime scene to collect forensic evidence, and the body can be the most important part of the evidence. Detective Martin's and Investigator Barnes' expertise in this matter was invaluable.

The Investigation

Documented from
U.S. Customs Criminal
Case File DR05BE465002

The Investigation

On January 26, 1984, Jesus Ramirez, Samuel Olguin, Rafael Calderon, and Ricardo Velazquez collectively decided to leave El Paso, Texas, and travel to the Del Rio area. They were all heroin addicts and were looking for ways to feed their habit. They spent the night at the Casa Blanca Motel in Comstock, Texas, and the following day, January 27, drove on to Del Rio in a 1975 white Pontiac Gran Prix, recently purchased from a party in El Paso. They crossed into Ciudad Acuña, Coahuila, Mexico and had lunch at the Los Arcos Restaurant. After eating, Ramirez left the group for approximately 30 minutes and upon his return, informed the others that he had located a jewelry store they could rob.

The jewelry store was identified as Varzu, S.A., located at Calle Lerdo #110 Sur. S.A. stands for Sociedad Anonima in the Spanish language, which literally translates "Anonymous Society," like our American "corporation." At approximately 3:30 p.m., Olguin, Ramirez, and Calderon entered the store. Olguin was armed with a Ruger Blackhawk .357-caliber revolver. The three robbed the store at gunpoint, taking an estimated $45,000 worth of gold jewelry. During the robbery, Velazquez remained with the Pontiac vehicle. Ramirez, Olguin, and Calderon returned to the vehicle and they drove to the POE at Del Rio. While enroute to the Port of Entry, the jewelry, taken in the robbery, was hidden by the perpetrators under the back seat of their vehicle.

At approximately 4:15 p.m., the Pontiac, containing the four men, entered the POE at Del Rio. Incarnacion Villareal, an Immigration Inspector, was stationed at the Primary

Checkpoint and asked the occupants about their citizenship. Ramirez, Olguin, and Calderon displayed proper identification and were admitted. Velasquez did not have any identification to prove citizenship other than a baptismal certificate. Inspector Villarreal referred the vehicle to a Secondary Checkpoint to have Velasquez's citizenship checked further.

Richard Latham was the Customs Inspector in Secondary who took charge of the vehicle. Latham took Velasquez into the Immigration Office and turned him over to Immigration Inspector Mario Zertuche. Zertuche examined Velasquez, admitted him, and turned him back to Latham who escorted him back to the Pontiac vehicle. Latham asked the remaining three to exit the vehicle and Latham began a routine inspection of the vehicle. Latham opened the trunk of the vehicle and searched for contraband. Latham then entered the driver's side of the vehicle and looked into the rear seat area. He then climbed into the back seat area of the vehicle and searched under the seat, discovering the stolen jewelry taken in the robbery. At this point, Ramirez entered the vehicle in the front passenger seat and displayed his .357 revolver, pointed it at Latham, and ordered him to sit down and shut up. The remaining three entered the vehicle while Ramirez held Latham at gunpoint.

The four, as well as Inspector Latham still being held at gunpoint, left the Port of Entry in the Pontiac and drove through Del Rio toward Eagle Pass, Texas, on Highway 277. While they were enroute toward Eagle Pass, Inspector Latham's service revolver and handcuffs were taken from him. Richard was handcuffed and held in the back seat. They drove approximately 52 miles from the Port of Entry, south on Highway 277.

They had been discussing whether they should kill Richard because they did not want to drive through Eagle Pass with a uniformed officer that everybody was looking for. They had this discussion in Spanish, which Richard understood and it must have caused Richard a lot of torment. They finally agreed they would kill Richard and stopped the vehicle near Elm Creek and took Richard out of the car. Ramirez and Calderon took Richard into an arroyo (ditch) on the side of the road and placed him face down on the ground. In statements taken from Velasquez and Olguin, each said that Calderon had Richard's service revolver and Ramirez still had the .357-caliber Ruger.

Both Velasquez and Olguin stated that they observed Calderon point the service revolver toward Richard's back. Two shots were fired into his back. It was later determined by investigating officers that the first shot entered his upper back, just left of center. This bullet was later found at autopsy to be lodged in his spine, just below the base of the neck. The second shot entered Richard's back approximately seven inches below the first shot, also left of the centerline of the back. This shot traveled through the body, penetrated, and passed through the heart and lodged just beneath the skin above the breastbone. In their statements, both Olguin and Velasquez say that there was a period of about 15 to 20 seconds between shots. After Richard was shot, both Ramirez and Calderon returned to the vehicle. Ramirez had Richard's wallet, Mace tear gas spray, and keys.

Investigators and medical examiners involved in this incident stated that Richard did not suffer much pain because of the location and rapidity of the wounds causing death.

The four left the murder scene in the Pontiac and drove to Eagle Pass, Texas, and proceeded into Piedras Negras, Mexico, just across the river from Eagle Pass and procured two rooms at the Autel Rio, rooms 208 and 209. During the evening hours, they got rid of the inexpensive costume jewelry and scored some heroin. Their plan was to split up with Olguin and Velasquez, taking the Pontiac back to Juarez through Mexico but neither had proper ownership papers for the vehicle and they were not granted permits by Mexican Officials to take the vehicle into the interior of Mexico. They subsequently traveled back to Ciudad Juarez through Mexico by train. Ramirez and Calderon took all the jewelry as well as the Ruger .357 revolver and Richard's service revolver and planned to take a taxi back into the U.S. at Eagle Pass the next day.

On the morning of January 28, 1984, Ramirez and Calderon contacted Amado Cantu-Mendez, a taxi driver from Piedras Negras, driving for Sitio Victoria, a cab company. Cantu took Ramirez and Calderon across the border to the Tampa Bar, 486 Jefferson Street, Eagle Pass. The two offered Cantu $200 to take them to El Paso, Texas. Cantu declined the offer because he did not hire out for long trips. As they were getting out of the taxi, Cantu observed a revolver with brown wooden grips in the waistband of one of the suspects.

Upon arrival in Eagle Pass, Ramirez and Calderon went to the Painter Bus Station in an attempt to get a bus back to El Paso. They found the bus station closed and walked toward the Trailways Bus Station. While en-route to the Trailways Station, an unidentified U.S. Border Patrol Officer allegedly stopped them for questioning. At this time, the suspects had not been identified and they were released by the officer after presenting proper citizenship identification.

At this point, Calderon and Ramirez rent-ed Room #9 at the Lane Motel in Eagle Pass. Later that morning, they discovered the earliest bus leaving for El Paso would not depart Eagle Pass until 3:30 p.m. that afternoon. They contacted Benigno Botello, a local taxi owner, and offered him $200 to take them to Presidio, Texas, with the idea that when they reached Marfa, Texas, they would offer Botello an additional $100 to take them on to El Paso. Botello agreed and he, Ramirez, and Calderon departed Eagle Pass in Botello's maroon four-door Ford Granada sedan.

They traveled west on Highway 277, pass-ing through law enforcement checkpoints. Law enforcements' attention was directed toward eastbound traffic and they were not detected. They traveled through Del Rio and then on Highway 90 through Comstock, Langtry, and west toward El Paso.

At approximately 12:35 p.m., Texas Department of Public Safety Troopers Jose Arturo Corral and Esequil Rodarte stopped the vehicle operated by Botello and occupied by Ramirez and Calderon between Langtry and Dryden. Corral and Rodarte had been alerted to the suspected abduction of Inspector Latham and had maintained a roadblock on Highway 90. Court decisions at that time mandated that roadblocks could only be maintained for a specific time period and now the officers were making investigative stops of all suspicious vehicles. Troopers Rodarte and Corral stopped Botello's vehicle approximately 15 miles west of Langtry, Texas, on U.S. Highway 90.

The Troopers identified all the occupants of the vehicle but were not able to contact their communications center because of the remote location. They also were not able to check for any warrants on the occupants of the Botello vehicle. The Troopers released the vehicle and moved to a location where they could contact their communications center. When they were able to establish radio communication, the Troopers learned of a possible warrant outstanding for Ramirez.

The Troopers relocated the Botello vehicle just east of Dryden, Texas, which is about 100 miles west of Del Rio and stopped it again. Botello jumped out of the car and ran to the Troopers claiming there was something wrong with the guys in the car. Trooper Corral approached the Botello vehicle from the right rear side and verbally requested, as well as signaled, the occupants to exit the vehicle. Trooper Rodarte covered Corral from the DPS marked unit. Trooper Corral observed that Ramirez was slouched down in the rear seat and also noticed movement by Ramirez.

It was at this time that a gunshot was fired from inside the vehicle. Both Troopers then observed blood on the right rear passenger side window of the Botello vehicle, caused by "blow back" from a contact wound. The Troopers made Calderon exit the vehicle and they took him into custody. A search of his body disclosed a pillowcase containing gold jewelry concealed in his crotch area.

This traffic stop became an issue of "cause" in a Motion to Suppress Hearing in Calderon's judicial proceedings but it was determined that since the Botello vehicle was a "public conveyance under hire," the only person who had "cause to suppress the evidence" was Botello, the owner of the taxi cab. This was critical to the prosecution because if the stop was suppressed, all the evidence in the vehicle—Richard's service revolver, the murder weapon, and the jewelry taken in the armed robbery found on the defendants—would not have been admissible in court.

After securing the scene, the Troopers discovered that Ramirez had shot himself in the right side of his head. Ramirez still had the

Ruger .357-caliber revolver in his right hand when the Troopers approached him. The Troopers also discovered that Ramirez was dead due to the gunshot wound to the head. It was determined that the bullet entered the right temple area of the deceased and passed through the skull, exiting the head in the area above the rear of the left ear. The bullet then exited the vehicle through the roof. It is theorized that Ramirez was going to try to shoot the Troopers and was holding the revolver in his right hand up against the side of his head with the hammer cocked. When he reached over with his left hand to open the rear door of the vehicle, the weapon discharged.

The Troopers found a Smith & Wesson .38-caliber Model 36 revolver in the back seat of the Botello vehicle which was later identified as Latham's service revolver. The five-shot revolver had two empty chambers.

During a pat down search of Calderon, Trooper Corral found a white pillowcase full of gold jewelry shoved down the front of Calderon's pants. Troopers Rodarte and Corral secured the scene until assistance arrived.

Special Agent Don Mog responded to the scene along with many other law enforcement officers. Because a shooting had occurred during a Texas DPS vehicle stop and apprehension, Texas Rangers were also in attendance.

At approximately 4:00 p.m., FBI Special Agent Moses Alaniz and District Attorney Investigator William Barnes arrived at the scene of the shooting by DPS helicopter. The scene was processed and agent Alaniz took into custody the Ruger .357 revolver, Latham's service revolver, the pillowcase with jewelry, and the personal effects of the deceased Ramirez and suspect Calderon. Investigator Barnes removed the body of Ramirez from the Botello vehicle and discovered a second white pillowcase, also full of gold jewelry, shoved down the front of Ramirez's pants. The jewelry was later identified as that taken in the armed robbery in Acuña.

It was later reported to me that, while the arrest scene at Dryden was being processed, the murder weapon, Richard's service revolver, had been placed on the trunk of the taxi along with the jewelry and other evidence. It was alleged that an unknown officer picked up the murder weapon stating, "Oh, is this the murder weapon?" Subsequently, it was determined that Calderon's fingerprints were not found on the weapon which caused a lot of consternation as we approached prosecution. Enough said!

Investigator Barnes placed Rafael Calderon under arrest for the aggravated kidnapping of Inspector Latham. The arrest was made without a warrant, but upon word from creditable individuals and to prevent the escape of defendant Calderon. Calderon was taken before Justice of the Peace Jannie McDonald, Precinct 2, Terrell County, Sanderson, Texas, and was read his rights by the magistrate. McDonald set Calderon's bond at $250,000. Texas Ranger Tol Dawson and FBI agent Alaniz transported Calderon back to Del Rio. In a sworn statement given to FBI Agent Alaniz, Calderon readily admitted he was involved in the jewelry store robbery and the kidnapping of the Customs Officer but he claimed that the one who killed Richard was Ramirez, the one in the back of the taxi with a hole in his head. Investigating officers did not quite believe his story and the investigation ensued.

Upon arrival in Val Verde County, it was discovered that the United States Attorney, San Antonio, had authorized a complaint filed against Calderon for Assault on a Federal Officer. As a result of this authorization, custody of Calderon was given over to federal authorities.

As an aside, Dryden, Texas, was the scene of the capture of the infamous "Caveman Bandit" by Terrill County Sheriff Bill Cooksey and Texas Ranger Alfred Allee, Jr. back in the 1960s. The bandit was Alfredo Hernandez, a Mexican illegal alien who terrorized ranchers, business owners, and the populace from Garner State Park near Uvalde, Texas, and over to Dryden, Texas. Hernandez started out sneaking into residences and businesses, stealing food and supplies to sustain himself while hiding in the many caves in that area of Texas, and traveling the country on the Southern Pacific Railroad system. He eventually shot and wounded Pelham Bradford, owner of the Pumpville Country Store and shot and wounded Sheriff Cooksey while the Sheriff and some citizens attempted to apprehend the bandit at a cave on the Deaton Ranch near Dryden. Full details of this saga can be found in the book *The Gun that Wasn't There* by Russell Smith, a retired Texas Police Chief.

On January 28, 1984, shortly before the activities in and near Dryden, Texas, occurred, the deceased body of Inspector Latham was discovered near Eagle Pass, Texas, near Elm Creek by Mr. Donaciano Vara-Salinas who was cutting firewood from the trees alongside the west side of U.S. Highway 277, approximately eight miles north of Eagle Pass. Vara was putting the wood in the back of his pickup when he observed a body in the roadside ditch, later identified as that of Inspector Latham. He contacted the Maverick County Sheriff's Office and notified them that he had spotted a body and its location. The first officer to arrive on the scene was Maverick County Sheriff's Deputy Alejandro Guedea who contacted Maverick County Justice of the Peace Rogelio Escobedo. Escobedo arrived at the scene and pronounced the body dead at 11:35 a.m.

A short time later, U.S. Customs, FBI, DPS, and Border Patrol Agents and I arrived at the scene as well as Val Verde County District Attorney Tom Lee. Assistant U.S. Attorney Danny Maeso arrived by Border Patrol helicopter from San Antonio. It was decided that Del Rio Police Officer Donald Weaver, the most experienced forensic investigator in the area, would process the crime scene assisted by other agents.

Too many investigators in a crime scene can compromise the collection of evidence, especially a homicide scene where you usually only get one chance. If you don't get it then, it is usually gone forever. Weaver had been requested by the FBI the previous evening to cross into Acuña, accompanied by Del Rio PD Detective Luis Robles, at the request of Mexican authorities, to process the robbery scene. This was a common occurrence in Del Rio as well as other border communities. In communities existing in isolated areas along the border with American and Mexican citizens who are related, when emergencies occur, they help one another for the common good. It was not unusual to see Del Rio fire engines and ambulances responding to emergencies in Acuña.

At 2:49 p.m., Latham's body was approximated (to estimate time of death), and Officer Weaver took photographs of Richard's body which was lying on his stomach with his hands handcuffed behind his back. It was observed on the body of Inspector Latham that there were two bullet holes. The hole closest to the hem of his Customs Duty jacket displayed some evidence of powder tattooing while the bullet entry closer to the head of the deceased did not. After processing the body and the area around the body for evidence, the body was removed. It was very apparent Richard had been killed execution style because he was handcuffed behind his back.

Both the body of Richard Latham and the body of Jesus Ramirez were transported to the Bexar County Medical Examiner's Office in San Antonio, Texas, for the purpose of post-mortem examination and the collection of evidence pursuant to the orders of the Justices of the Peace who pronounced them dead.

During this period, I was advised by my secretary, Dorothy Nell Davis, who was in charge of the command center at our office, that Customs Commissioner William Von Raab had called numerous times but I was busy in the field. When I finally spoke to the Commissioner, he asked if I had enough help on the investigation. I informed Commissioner Von Raab that we had enough manpower but could use the assistance of Customs Air Support Units to cover the vast area where the investigation seemed to be headed. Commissioner Von Raab simply told me that whatever I needed from Customs assets I could have it. This meant a lot to me as an employee of the U.S. Customs Service and renewed the feeling that we in Customs were a family—something that doesn't exist in other agencies.

Also during this period, I received many telephone calls from Customs Officers who were friends of Richard's and some that did not know him, volunteering their time to assist in the investigation.

At another time on an unrelated case, Commissioner Von Raab sealed the Mexican border when Drug Enforcement Agency (DEA) Special Agent Kiki Camarena was kidnapped and murdered in Guadalajara, Mexico years later. Commissioner Von Raab's action during that tragic incident will alway hold him in high regard by DEA agents and the Department of Justice. Imagine the millions of vehicles and foot traffic across the Mexican border on a daily basis and the effect of totally stopping traffic for about a 24-hour period; the residual commercial effects on the economy on both sides of the border were huge. But you have to do what you have to do when a federal agent is murdered and the Commissioner of Customs had that power. Full details of that investigation can be found in *O Plata O Plomo? (Silver or Lead)* by retired Border Patrolman/Customs/DEA Agent James Kuykendall.

On January 29, 1984, the autopsy on Richard Latham began at 8:00 a.m. in the Bexar County Medical Examiner's Office, San Antonio, Texas. I did not attend because I had no experience in those matters and I did not think I could be present at an autopsy of a friend of mine. Those present for the autopsy were Dr. Suzanna Dana, FBI Agent Claude Martin, Detectives Martin and Lt. Daniel Cruz, of the Del Rio Police Department. In addition, Corporal T.J. Jagge from the San Antonio

Police Department was present to assist with the processing of any items that might present fingerprint evidence. It was determined that Richard had died as a result of two bullet wounds to the back—one severing the spinal cord and one passing through his heart. (We did not know any of this until the Bureau of Alcohol, Tobacco, and Firearms (ATF) came back with the ballistic results.) It was determined Richard's hands were shackled with his own handcuffs.

After completing the autopsy of Richard Latham, Dr. Dana began the autopsy of a male subject then identified as Jesus Ramirez-Reyes. During Dr. Dana's preliminary examination of the body, Detective Martin removed three gold rings from the deceased's hands and a gold chain from around his neck. Bexar County Medical Examiner's Office Laboratory Technician Gilbert Escalona performed a test for gunshot residue on Ramirez's hands.

Dr. Dana then performed the autopsy. The external examination by Dr. Dana showed the body had a contact gunshot wound to the right upper temple area. The examination also revealed an exit wound above and behind the left ear of Ramirez. Lt. Cruz took photographs of both autopsies. Lt. Cruz also took into evidence both bullets recovered by Dr. Dana from Richard Latham's body.

On January 29, 1984, Rafael Calderon was taken before U.S. Magistrate Durwood Edwards in Del Rio and a complaint was filed for violations of assault and murder of a federal employee. Magistrate Edwards advised Calderon of his rights in the matter and set bond at $250,000. Calderon was unable to execute a bond and was committed to the Val Verde County Jail to be held in federal custody.

During this time, my secretary, Dorothy Nell Davis, a longtime resident of Del Rio and a native Texan, advised me that the word around town was that some of the locals were talking about administering some "West Texas Justice" on the shooter, Calderon. The Val Verde County Jail was then located in the courthouse and the Sheriff's Department consisted of only a few deputies. It was theorized that it would be easy to overpower them and dispense the justice that a lot of the locals deemed appropriate. Richard was a hometown boy who was loved and respected by many. Calderon was subsequently moved to the Maverick County Jail in Eagle Pass for his protection.

Another matter that came up during that time was that the local attorneys who could be court appointed to defend Calderon did not want to defend the man who shot Richard Latham because it would ruin their reputations. They complained that they had to continue to live and practice law in the Del Rio area and it would impact their practices.

On January 29, 1984, DEA Agent Art Rodriguez, Eagle Pass, received information from Mexican Officials that the Pontiac vehicle operated by Ramirez, Calderon, Velasquez, and Olguin had been located in the parking lot of the Charleston Club, located at the corner of Allende and Zaragosa Streets in Piedras Negras across the river from Eagle Pass. Agent Rodriguez also was informed by Mexican Officials that Richard Latham's wallet, mace, a spent Plus P .38 cartridge, some car keys, and documents had been turned into Mexican Police by two residents of Piedras Negras. These residents reported to Mexican Police that they had found the items in a vacant lot on the east side of the stadium, located at the corner of Salubridad and Liberacion streets in Piedras Negras.

Upon learning of these discoveries, Agent Rodriguez and Customs Special Agent Larry Valigura began making arrangements to have the items turned over to United States Authorities. The cartridge was subsequently identified as being fired from Richard's service revolver. Included in the documents were traffic tickets and other papers that led to the identification of Ricardo Velasquez in El Paso and Samuel Olguin in Juarez.

A certain amount of money was paid to Mexican Officials for the recovery of this important evidence. This may come as a shock to many of you because we, here in the U.S., would never have to "buy" evidence from another police agency. Those of us who have worked on the border understand. It is a different culture based on roots in early Europe where the "bite" or "mordida" is just a way of doing business. I found this especially distasteful considering this case involved a fellow Customs Officer and a personal friend of mine. Additionally, it was repulsive because of the hours and hours of liaison conducted with the Mexicans while I was on the border and the billions of dollars that this country has pumped into the Mexican anti-drug effort all these years.

During the period of January 30, 1984 through February 2, 1984, a major effort was exerted by various law enforcement agencies to locate Velasquez and Olguin. The search was made throughout Texas with a concerted effort in El Paso, Texas, and Ciudad Juarez, Mexico, as the result of physical and documentary evidence found in the vehicle in Piedras Negras and extensive record checks and investigation. These leads were forwarded to Dennis Derr, Special Agent in Charge of our El Paso Office. Teams of Customs, FBI, and other law enforcement agents were assigned to follow up the investigation. SAC Derr reported, "The cooperation with my counterpart, FBI SAC Richard Holverson, was fantastic."

On February 3, 1984, Special Agents from the U.S. Customs Service and FBI located Velasquez in room #7 of the Star Dust Motel in El Paso, Texas, and took him into custody. Investigators had determined that Velasquez had been calling his girlfriend in El Paso and they obtained cooperation from her and her family to install a "Tap and Trace" on their telephone which lead to Velasquez's arrest. A Trap and Trace device can be installed on a cooperating person's telephone by court order. Basically, how it works is when an incoming call rings, it traps the caller's signal and keeps the line open. The telephone company then traces the incoming call to its origin.

On February 4, 1984, Detective Martin, Investigator Barnes, Customs Special Agent Dave Barela, and I interviewed Ricardo Velasquez in the U.S. Attorney's office in El Paso. Velasquez admitted his involvement in the armed robbery and kidnapping of Inspector Latham and implicated Ramirez, Calderon, and Olguin. Velasquez further stated he thought Ramirez may have shot Latham but actually did not see him do it. Martin, Barnes, and I later transported Velasquez back to Del Rio on a Customs aircraft and he was turned over to U.S. Deputy Marshal Jim Lee who placed Velasquez in confinement in the Maverick County Jail in Eagle Pass.

On February 5, 1984, Samuel Olguin contacted Federal Authorities in the U.S. and surrendered himself at the Port of Entry at El Paso. Information had been provided to the Mexican Direccion Federal Seguridad (DFS) which is supposedly similar to our Secret Service, but in reality are the "political police" in Mexico. The only thing similar to our Secret Service is they protect Mexican government dignitaries in power. From my experience with them, I would classify them as nothing more than "thugs" who have the "Carta Blanca" (white card) which could include political assassination. The DFS had been conducting a series of fact-finding raids on residences of anybody remotely connected to Olguin, which probably included kicking down doors and beating up people. Note: It is their country and they can operate any way they want to. But...as a result, Olguin's family finally convinced him to turn himself in. It was reported Oluguin telephoned the Port of Entry at El Paso, identified himself, requested that nobody shoot him, and then he walked across the International Bridge and surrendered to Customs authorities. This necessitated another Customs Aircraft trip to El Paso but I did not mind. The Customs Air Branch in San Antonio was providing a Beech

200 King Air which is pressurized and a nice way to "go through the air."

On February 10, 1984, Calderon, Olguin, and Velasquez were taken before U.S. Magistrate Durwood Edwards in Del Rio and a preliminary hearing was held to determine if sufficient probable cause existed to bind the defendants over for consideration by the Federal Grand Jury. After hearing evidence, Magistrate Edwards found sufficient probable cause and ordered the defendants held until their case could be considered by the Grand Jury.

On that date, Investigator Benny Davis, Bureau of Alcohol, Tobacco, and Firearms (ATF), San Antonio, initiated a gun trace on the .357 Ruger Black Hawk. He subsequently determined L.M. Burney, a licensed gun dealer in La Mesa, Texas, had received the weapon from Ruger Arms Company on September 14, 1971. Approximately three weeks later, the gun was noticed to be missing from their inventory. A local contractor, Jack Lauderdale, was doing repair work on the warehouse door and Burney thinks one of his helpers probably stole it. Lauderdale was subsequently contacted and could find no record that any of the defendants had worked for him.

On February 21, 1984, the Federal Grand Jury in Del Rio, Texas ,returned a six count indictment against defendants Calderon, Velasquez, and Olguin for violations of Aiding and Abetting, Assaulting, Resisting or Impeding Certain Officers or Employees of the U.S., Conspiracy, Smuggling Goods into the U.S., Flight to Avoid Prosecution, and Transportation of Stolen Goods. Calderon was also indicted for Assault and Murder of a Federal Employee.

On February 29, 1984, FBI Special Agent Weathermon, Investigator Barnes, Detectives Martin, Armando Ramirez, and I interviewed Olguin, accompanied by his attorney, Humberto Garcia, in the Kinney County Jail in Brackettville, Texas. Olguin now put Latham's gun in Calderon's hand and said he saw Calderon shooting Latham. He also stated he and the others left El Paso with the intentions of pulling armed robberies to get money for heroin. In fact, he stated he, Calderon, and Ramirez robbed "La Italia" money exchange store in Juarez, Mexico about a week prior to coming to Del Rio for the same reason.

On March 8, 1984, Assistant U.S. Attorney Danny Maeso advised that ballistics tests by ATF confirmed both bullets recovered from Inspector Latham's body had been fired from his own weapon. Additionally, the spent .38-caliber Plus P cartridge case found with Latham's wallet in Piedras Negras had been fired by Latham's gun.

On March 12, 1984, Special Agent Weathermon advised that fingerprint analysis showed drug arrests for Calderon and Ricard Velasquez-Cortez and an assault arrest for Calderon by the El Paso Police Department.

On March 13, 1984, Velasquez and Olguin were indicted by the Val Verde County Grand

Jury, Del Rio, Texas, for Aggravated Kidnap.

On March 15, 1984, Calderon was indicted by the Maverick County Grand Jury, Eagle Pass, Texas, for Capital Kidnap-Murder.

On March 22, 1984, Investigator Barnes, Detective Martin, and I interviewed Velasquez in the Maverick County Jail. Velasquez stated that he had previously given a statement to us on February 4, 1984. He was giving this statement now because he did not tell everything he knew in the first statement and his lawyer had advised him to tell the police officers the entire story. No one had told him that he would get any special treatment or a lesser sentence for giving a statement.

He first met Rafael Calderon in an alley in El Paso, Texas. Calderon used to hang around with a group known as the "Blue Stars" which used to get together and play basketball in an alley. On January 26, 1984, Calderon, Ramirez, Olguin and he were together and Ramirez suggested they should all go to San Antonio, Texas, to look for work. Ramirez said that if they couldn't find work, they could rob some places to get some money for heroin. They all left that day around 6:30 p.m. and drove until about 3 a.m. the next morning. They stopped in a small town near Del Rio and got a motel room. On the trip, Ramirez had a gun and so did Olguin. Ramirez had a big black gun and Olguin had a small chrome gun. While they were in the motel room, they all shot up with heroin. They got up the next morning and drove to Ciudad Acuña, Mexico. They got there about 3 or 3:30 p.m. They ate, and afterward, Ramirez and Calderon walked off by themselves. They came back about 30 minutes later and Ramirez said that he had found a store to rob.

The robbery of the store and the kidnapping of Inspector Latham went just like Velasquez said in his first statement. The only differences were: When they left the Port of Entry in Del Rio, he got in the back seat next to Latham. He took the handcuffs out of the case on Latham's gun belt and tried to put them on Latham but couldn't.

Ramirez took a handkerchief out of his own pocket and took the handcuffs from him using the handkerchief so he wouldn't get his fingerprints on the handcuffs. Ramirez then handcuffed Latham's hands behind his back. When they got near Eagle Pass, Calderon pulled the car over to the side of the road. Calderon got Latham out of the back of the car and he and Ramirez took Latham down into the arroyo beside the highway. He and Olguin got out of the car and watched what they were doing. He saw Calderon with a gun in his hand. It was smaller than the one that Ramirez had and he thought it was Latham's gun.

He did not remember who took Latham's gun while they were in the car but he did know that he noticed that the gun was missing from Latham's holster while they were driving toward Eagle Pass. He watched Calderon point the gun at Latham's back and he turned away.

Just as he turned away, he heard a shot. He looked back at Latham and saw Calderon still pointing the gun at Latham. He then saw Calderon fire a second shot into Latham's back. Calderon then put the gun in his pants as he and Ramirez walked back to the car. Calderon got in the driver's side and they drove to Piedras Negras, Mexico where they rented rooms. The rest of the story is just like he said in his first statement. They split up with Calderon and Ramirez keeping all the jewelry and the two guns.

To those of us in law enforcement, we know that you never get the whole truth during interviews and statements of defendants, especially when the crime is murder. Defendants always try to minimize their involvement, and in this case, nobody wanted to admit they were even sitting next to Richard on the drive from Del Rio to the murder scene. For those of you who have been paying close attention to this investigation, the chrome derringer weapon reportedly carried by Olguin was never recovered.

On April 5, 1984, Velasquez and Olguin pled guilty to charges on a plea agreement of 30 years for their involvement in the kidnapping murder of Inspector Latham. Sentencing was held in abeyance until the completion of the federal murder trial of Rafael Calderon, tentatively set for May 14, 1984 in San Antonio. Velasquez and Olguin still faced aggravated kidnap charges in Val Verde County. Calderon still faced capital kidnap-murder charges in Maverick County.

On April 13, 1984, Customs Special Agent Barela of our El Paso Office interviewed Mr. Ruben Gonzalez, who was the victim of an assault by Calderon and gang members. Mr. Gonzalez immediately and without hesitation identified Calderon in the photo spread. Gonzalez stated that during the assault, he was the proprietor of the Frontera Bar, 601 S. El Paso Street, El Paso, Texas. Gonzalez said that on six or seven occasions Calderon had burglarized the premises, stealing beer and liquor. Gonzalez described further actions of Calderon as vandalizing the bar's restroom by kicking at the tile wall, bringing in beer from outside the premises, and smoking marijuana.

Gonzalez said Calderon would cause numerous disturbances with bar patrons. At times, Gonzalez said he would have to escort the bar patrons to their vehicles to avoid Calderon's hostile actions. Specifically, on two occasions, Gonzalez stated he had a violent confrontation with Calderon. On the second occasion, Calderon, along with some of his friends, severely beat Gonzalez using a pool cue stick and kicked him causing fractures and lacerations. Mr. Gonzalez advised that Calderon portrayed himself as the lead force in the gang's congregation.

Also on April 13, Agent Barela interviewed the proprietor of La Italia Money Exchange and Jewelry Store in Ciudad Juarez, Mexico. The proprietor, the victim of a January 13, 1984 armed robbery, failed to identify any of the kidnap-murder suspects in a photo spread. The victim stated he was robbed by three Mexican individuals—two holding pistols and the third a knife. Among the items taken were jewelry, money, and a .38-caliber chrome plated two shot derringer. The victim advised that he believed the subjects were from the El Paso area because of their speech mannerisms.

Further criminal checks revealed Rafael Calderon had been arrested by the El Paso Police Department on April 23, 1979 for theft, with no disposition known. The El Paso P.D. also arrested him on February 14, 1980. This charge was dropped, and he was convicted on June 10, 1980 for criminal mischief and given one year probation. He was arrested on June 29, 1983 for possession of marijuana (under 2.02 ounces) and there was no disposition yet. Ricardo Velasquez was arrested December 6, 1982 by El Paso P.D. for possession of marijuana and the matter was still pending. Samuel Olguin was arrested August 21, 1982 for driving while intoxicated and carrying a weapon; no disposition was known at that time.

During the course of the investigation, Tol Dawson, Texas Ranger stationed in Del Rio, came to my office and expressed regret and anguish that all three were not being prosecuted for capital murder. District Attorney Lee advised that under Texas State Law at that time in capital cases, each defendant's actions were the determining factor of charges and you could not seek the death penalty unless you could prove a "continuing pattern or propensity to commit further violent actions." DA Lee pointed out that you do not prosecute weak capital murder cases because it leads to problems for future prosecutions.

Also during the course of this investigation, approximately 70 pieces of physical and documentary evidence were seized—evidence which, as indicated before, solidified the theory that Ramirez, Calderon, Velasquez, and Olguin conspired to commit the robbery and kill Inspector Latham. Documents found at the Dryden scene and on Ramirez and Calderon implicated and eventually led to the capture of Velasquez and Olguin. Collecting, analyzing, and reporting the volume of documentary evidence was a Herculean chore while writing the criminal case report, but I refuse to bother the reader with those details. Suffice it to say that the documents tied the conspirators together, led to the capture of the perpetrators, and justice was served.

June 5, 1984, Olguin and Velasquez pled guilty before Texas District Judge George M. Thurmond in Del Rio as a result of a plea agreement between Olguin's attorney Humberto Garcia and Velasquez's attorney Rufino Cabello, along with the district attorney's office.

On August 31, 1984, the shooter, Calderon, pled guilty before Judge Sessions in San Antonio Federal District Court. The hearing took approximately one an one-half hours because of federal regulations and safeguards for defendant's rights. The subsequent plea in State Court only took five minutes. When this case was over, I felt a large degree of accomplishment and relief from the stress of an investigation that was under the microscope of the Del Rio community and that of my agency. I was pretty much burned out.

Many others assisted in this investigation but I would like to acknowledge Senior Special Agent Pat Woods of our El Paso office who assisted in the capture of Velasquez and Olguin. We had a lot of luck on this investigation but I believe it was generated by those of us involved going 24 hours a day until the violators were apprehended in such a short tine. We made our own "luck."

In 2002, this case was profiled for the television program *FBI Files,* and subsequently many persons have remarked to me, "Gosh, I saw you on T.V." or "I didn't know you did that for a living!" The program was produced for the FBI by New Dominion Pictures of Suffolk, Virginia. The program was a reenactment of the Latham case and investigation. At the time, I was training the new Transportation Security Administration (TSA) Baggage Screeners and was traveling between Los Angeles, Boston, Cleveland, and other cities as an Instructor for Advanced Integrated Systems out of Renton, Washington.

It was impossible for me to attend the filming in San Antonio but I was finally interviewed for the program in Denver in January, 2003. When I was initially contacted by New Dominion, they asked me what I looked like back in 1984. Self-effacing humor has never been my short suit, so I told them back in 1984 I thought I looked like Sam Elliot, the actor. But in 2003, I probably looked more like the late actor Wilfred Brimley, the Quaker Oats champion on television commercials and Robert Redford's cantankerous manager in the baseball movie *The Natural*. I have enjoyed the work of these two fine actors for many years.

As stated, the FBI played an important role in this investigation and, considering it was their program, I thought they treated the U.S. Customs Service fairly well, but as usual, they were depicted as doing most everything. Those of us who were directly involved in the investigation know who did what and that is the important thing. Richard Latham, a U.S.

Customs Inspector, was kidnapped from a U.S. Government facility while on duty protecting this country and was brutally murdered execution style. Through the concerted outstanding efforts of many law enforcement agencies, the perpetrators were apprehended in a short period of time and prosecuted to the fullest extent of the law.

Maybe if Richard had received the "street survival training" that law enforcement officers get today, he would still be alive. Street survival training was not available for Customs Inspectors in the '80s. This training consists of drilling into officers and agents to expect the unexpected and avoid complacency. And, in my opinion, survival training emphasizes that "You should never, never, ever give up and that you could place a government credit card over a sucking chest wound and keep on a-goin'." Richard had his life and destiny in his hands and just made the wrong decision based on his training or lack of it.

Sentencing

Remanded to the custody of the U.S. Attorney General

Sentencing

On September 28, 1984, the defendants were sentenced in U.S. District Court in San Antonio by Chief District Judge William S. Sessions. The shooter, Rafael Calderon, was sentenced to be imprisoned for life. Ricardo Velasquez and Samuel Olguin were sentenced to a total of 23 years, each sentence for the four count indictment to be served consecutively.

The federal government has a unique way of phrasing the sentencing in that defendants are remanded to the custody of the U.S. Attorney General, which means they will serve their tine in a federal prison without consideration for parole. You do the time the best way you can. Calderon was serving his life sentence at Leavenworth, Kansas. Velasquez was at El Reno, Oklahoma and Olguin was at Lompoc, Californina.

Epilogue

The tail that wagged the dog

Epilogue

During the investigation, I learned Richard's maternal grandfather, James Wallen, a mounted Customs Inspector at Del Rio, was killed in the line of duty by whiskey smugglers in 1923. Research disclosed the following information from The San Antonio Light newspaper dated March 7, 1923. Jim Wallen, a former Del Rio City Marshal, Texas Ranger, and Immigration Officer had left the Port of Entry at Del Rio after his "swing shift" at approximately 1:30 p.m. On his way home, he spotted a suspicious vehicle near the port and, on investigation, was fired on by suspects. Inspector Wallen returned fire but later died after a bullet pierced his heart. Subsequently, investigation disclosed he wounded one of the suspects evidenced by the trail of blood leading back to the Rio Grande River. One hundred quarts of tequila were seized and two suspects were arrested.

Tom Lee, the former District Attorney in Del Rio, is now the District Judge of the 63rd State District Court of Texas at Del Rio and the former Assistant U.S. Attorney, Dan Maeso is now in private practice in Montgomery, Texas. I cannot say enough about the legal expertise that these two gentlemen brought to this investigation. This matter involved jurisdictional situations between state and federal authorities, which were adjudicated only in the interest of finding who killed Richard and determining the best way to prosecute the offenders. It has been my experience that in most cases, the best attorneys eventually go on to judgeships and that is the case for Tom Lee.

In the case of Dan Maeso, it has been my experience that U.S. Attorney's Offices around the country are an excellent training ground for young, new attorneys fresh out of law school. They are able to get experience in criminal and civil law at a very high level. Some only stay for the experience and then move on to private practice for more money. Some stay and become professional government prosecutors because they enjoy enforcing the law instead of defending against it. Those readers who have experienced an investigation at the federal level will understand just how important those seasoned prosecutors are. Once a federal agency's ongoing case is presented to the U.S. Attorney's Office, they are really in charge of the investigation; it is a team effort on behalf of the United States Government and their legal input is very important to prepare the case for prosecution and eventual trial.

During the investigation, Judy Turner, a Customs Labor Employee Specialist from Houston, arrived in Del Rio to assist Richard's family through this terrible ordeal. Judy was the beginning of a new program in Customs called the Traumatic Incident Program, initiated by then Regional Commissioner of Customs, Donald Kelley, which eventually evolved into the Employee Assistance Program. This program assisted families of Customs employees who suffered a life tragedy involving death or serious injury and was assisted by the Roger Von Amelunxen Foundation which, at that time and until recently, provided grants and scholarships to the families of slain officers. The Foundation is no longer active, but the Employee Assistance Program was carried over to the new Department of Homeland Security agencies, Customs and Border Protection and Immigration Customs Enforcement during the giant merger after 9/11.

On January 31, 1984, a funeral service was held for Richard at Del Rio. Approximately 600 people stood in a light rain during the graveside services. Those in attendance included local, county, state, and federal officials and many of Richard's family and friends. Richard was a Mason and his funeral was concluded with Masonic Rites. W.E. Zorn, Masonic Lodge past master, officiated the rights at graveside. Zorn was a close family friend as well.

"It's like putting my own boy away," he said, wiping a tear from his eye. Zorn said his sons and Richard were friends since childhood. "I wouldn't let anyone else do it," he said, referring to his officiating Masonic Rites for Richard. Lawmen wearing uniforms of various law enforcement agencies were visible throughout the crowd of those in attendance at the graveside service. Delegations from the Del Rio Police Department, Fire Department, and Department of Public Safety troopers, Texas Rangers, Immigration and Naturalization Service, and U.S. Customs paid their respects to the family and memory of a fine man and loved officer.

Twenty-five years have passed since this terrible incident happened. I'm sure the idea to write a book about this case passed through my mind sometime after the emotional trauma was over. For many years I could not even look at the copy of the criminal case report I took with me when I left Del Rio on my way to Tucson, Arizona where I subsequently retired in 1996.

Occasionally,I would come across the file while looking through papers at the office or our family residence but it would bring back painful memories of a friend tragically lost and the creeping suspicion that if I had only reacted quicker or I had done something differently, I could have saved Richard.

During and after my career, I have talked to many law enforcement officers regarding this feeling of being responsible and sense of guilt for another officer's death because we just did not do enough nor do it fast enough. I struggled with this feeling for many years and had to get some professional help with this matter. It was not until 9/11 that I started to come to grips with this problem. I was able to reconnect with a number of old rascals with whom I used to work. Reflecting on the case and the work of the Von Amelunxen Foundation, I decided it was time to write this book and donate the proceeds, over and above expenses, to the Foundation. Sadly, the Foundation is no longer active, so I am donating proceeds from the sale of the new edition to the Tunnel to Towers Foundation.

I decided to dedicate this book to Richard and the men and women who "hold the line" on our borders and because of their dedication, help keep this country safe from criminals, drugs, and now terrorists.

While researching material for this book, I came in contact with Joaquin Jackson, a Texas Ranger who had been assigned to Uvalde, Texas, while I was in Del Rio. I had met Joaquin but our career paths did not intersect while I was in Texas. I had occasion to meet his son, Lance, who is a Border Patrol supervisor in Marfa, Texas, while I was doing security background investigations under contract for the new Customs and Border Protection outfit under Homeland Security. I learned that Joaquin was retired in Alpine, Texas, and was reminded that Joaquin had written two books, *One Ranger* and *One Ranger Returns*. I ordered these books and enjoyed them immensely. They were an inspiration and gave me the impetus to finish writing this book. The area of West Texas he covered in his career was similar to mine and the reading experience brought back old memories.

The Texas Rangers have a much-storied history having been founded in Texas to protect early settlers from Indians and Mexicans during the turbulent days of that state's foundation. The *One Ranger* title comes from a statement attributed to Ranger William McDonald who was sent to Dallas, Texas, in response to a request from city fathers concerned that a scheduled prize fight would result in riotous conditions. When Ranger McDonald stepped off the train, he was greeted by an anxious mayor who asked, "Where are the others?" To that McDonald reportedly replied, "Hell, ain't I enough? There's only one prizefight!"

This statement has been changed over the years to "one ranger, one riot," etc. but it exemplifies the courage and resolve of Texas Rangers throughout history. Also attributed to Ranger McDonald is another favorite saying of mine that has been established as a Ranger creed—"No man can stand up against a fellow that's in the right and keeps on a-comin'." Coincidentally, I worked with this Ranger's grandson, Bill McDonald, while I was in Del Rio and we have become good friends. Bill, like me, was a former Border Patrolman, Customs Agent and retired from DEA to Del Rio.

While in Del Rio, I worked with Texas Ranger Tol Dawson, previously identified in this book. I always thought that if I was ever in a tight scrape, I would want people like Tol with me. I also had the pleasure of working with Johnnie Aycock who, at the time, was a DPS Narcotics Sergeant in Del Rio. Johnnie went on to become a Texas Ranger and finished a very brave and courageous career. The stories can be read in *One Ranger*.

When I retired, I went out like many agents—disgusted with how our agency and others had changed in the 30 years I served. The Customs Agency Service I joined in 1970 did not bear any semblance to the outfit I retires from in 1996. When I became an agent in San Francisco in 1970, the job title was just "Customs Agent" and there were only about 400 agent's worldwide. Customs Agents were assigned to embassies around the world to conduct classification and value investigations relating to importations of goods. They were also in those foreign countries to gather drug interdiction efforts, We also handled all internal integrity investigations before the creation of an Internal Affairs Division.

We were referred to by other divisions of Customs as "The Tail that Wagged the Dog" because we handled all the criminal and significant enforcement business of Customs.

It is my opinion there are many reasons for the changes, one being the Customs Service seemed to reorganize internally every few years with divisions within the service seeking more manpower and jurisdiction, hence "super grades" for management positions within the agency. I always referred to this phenomenon as "empire building." Of course, other divisions of the service had always been jealous of "the agents" because we had ultimate authority in criminal case decisions, dressed in civilian clothes (formal and casual), and carried guns. We also had a government vehicle assigned to us, which we got to take home so that we would be able to respond directly to emergencies. And, to top it all off, we were reported to have a "cavalier" attitude about most everything.

The U.S. Customs Service, which was founded back in 1789, does not exist any more. After the Revolutionary War, this new nation adopted the British system of Customs, or Collections of Customs, which called for collecting revenue from import duties and fines for violations. Piracy and smuggling was a problem for the new nation as it was for the former colonies. The investigative arm of the Customs Service under the Treausury Department was founded by the first Secretary of the Treasury, Alexander Hamilton. He established a small cadre of auditors to make sure the Collectors of Customs did not have their hands in the federal cookie jar. I guess we all have a cross to bear and the fact that we were founded as a bunch of auditors is ours. This small outfit gradually evolved into the Customs Agency Service fro the days of Elliot Ness and the Treasury Agents.

It is now called Customs and Border Protection (CBP) which includes a division of the former U.S. Border Patrol and a combined agency of former Customs and Immigration Inspectors, all under the new agency created after 9/11, Homeland Security. The criminal investigators of Customs and Immigration were merged into Immigration Customs Enforcement (ICE). It is sad to me and many of my colleagues that this happened but time will tell just how effective these new agencies will be. As a new friend of mine, Dorothy Swartz, wrote in one of her country and western songs, "They are dancin' an old tune to a new country band."

Those of us who served on the border will always remember the espirit-de-corps and camaraderie that kept us together in the common cause of protecting our nation's borders—something of which I will always be proud. I now maintain camaraderie through membership in the Association of Former Customs Special Agents (AFCSA), the Fraternal Order of Retired Border Patrol Officers (FORBPO), and the Fraternal Order of Border Agents (FOBA), also known as "Border Rats."

There is also an informal group that seems to be a loose knit outfit of members from all three of these groups called "The Pecos Group" that meets in Del Rio around Halloween each year for fellowship and "adult libations." I have found I need this fellowship with many of my old compadres to maintain my sanity in today's world. Once you have been a member of an elite outfit, it is hard to just walk away from it. We are like firemen—some people run to a fire and some people run away from it. We are who our job is, to protect and serve.

In January, 1989, a tribute was paid to Richard at the Port of Entry at Del Rio, commemorating five years since this tragic incident. The tribute was attended by law enforcement officers from local, state, and federal agencies, local dignitaries, and the Regional Commissioner and District Director of the U.S. Customs Service.

As you might imagine, there were expectations of awards from the Customs Service to the men who went over and above the call of duty on this case. AUSA Daniel Maseo received the Commissioner's Award, *but they spelled his name wrong.* The Regional Commissioner's Office in Houston stated no agents would be recognized for their work on this case because "they were just doing their job." I believe this attitude resulted from the fact that Customs Investigations was now under the Regional Commissioner who had no respect or use for us older Customs Agents whom he referred to as "cowboys." We were not afraid to criticize "enforcement programs" initiated by Region, many of which left our dear agency with "egg on our faces."

For me, just Texas Ranger Tol Dawson coming by the office and telling me that the Texas Rangers thought the Customs Service did a good job on this case and the thanks from the Latham family was enough.

As far as I know, this is the first book about the Latham affair. During research for this book, I learned another former Customs official had given a chapter account of how he and other retired Customs officers had solved this case. It was included as a chapter in a rambling story about his life, military service, and life as a Customs Agent. The only problem with his account is that he dated his heroic actions in

1987, three years after the incident took place. Another fallacy is that he placed a retired Customs Agent, who served Customs and his nation with distinction, in a law enforcement position in Del Rio that he did not occupy in 1984.

Writing his account of the case in 1987 naturally gave him the benefit of the criminal case report we wrote in 1984, so naturally he did a sterling job of investigation. Many people have tried to take credit for capturing the ones that killed Richard. This account should set the record straight. I think it is natural for those of us who actually did the investigative work to resent the "armchair quarterbacks" who try to steal the credit for an investigation they had absolutely nothing to do with, except to come to Del Rio after the perpetrators were apprehended and get in everybody's way.

Del Rio Memories

*Stuff you now only
see in movies*

Del Rio Memories

In August, 1978, I was promoted to Resident Agent in Charge at Del Rio. Coming from my previous post in San Francisco was somewhat of a culture shock, but I had grown up in a small town farm and ranch community in the state of Washington, near the Canadian Border. I spoke Spanish as a result of my four and one-half years with the Border Patrol. I liked Mexican food, and dressed "western." I arrived in Del Rio with my wife (whom I always introduce as *"The Lovely Valerie")* and our two children—Erin, our daughter who was six and our son, Justin, who was just turning three. The only other agent at the office was Bob Gerber (who was later transferred to Houston.) Only later were Special Agents Robert Sam Hale and Donald Mog transferred to Del Rio.

We covered all the way to Midland and Odessa, and at times I was in charge of the Eagle Pass Office, which made me a Special Agent in Charge, although the office was a little one. Sam Swartz was my Special Agent in Charge at times in Laredo and San Antonio and Sam was my favorite boss, along with Harold C. "Bud" Olson, whom I worked with in San Francisco and for in Sacramento.

There have been many famous and storied Customs Agents who have served at Del Rio: Tom Dean, John Van Diver, Bill McGee, Jack Salter, and Cliff Wilson (chuckle), among others, and I consider it an honor to have been selected to serve in that little West Texas outpost.

My wife got a job teaching school at Sacred Heart Academy where our children attended until we transferred to Tucson in 1985. This started our friendship with George "Kip" and Margie Knutson. Kip is my favorite "Fighter Pilot." He trained in F-4s and went on to fly F-16s remote in Korea and finally a desk at the Pentagon. Margie was a teacher at Sacred Heart and Kip was an instructor pilot at Laughlin Air Force Base.

Dorothy Nell Davis was the secretary and our office was located just across the street from the Port of Entry. Dorothy was a character and everybody loved her. She was the recognized Customs expert in the nation regarding administrative procedures. We would get telephone calls from Houston, New York, Miami, Los Angeles, Seattle, and Chicago asking Dorothy how to handle some administrative problem.

Dorothy, a native Texan, had been a legal secretary for a law firm in San Antonio which handled oil and gas leases. She had also been the Comptroller at Laughlin AFB. She could take shorthand better than anyone I knew. She once recorded a meeting in my office with four people dictating and never missed a word. She was married to Jack "Roy" Davis who had an American National Insurance business in Del Rio for many years. Some Friday nights when Jack and "Ol' Dorothy," as he called her, were going out on the town, Dorothy Nell Davis would arrive at the office driving a Cadillac, wearing a mink stole or coat and dressed "to the nines." I always told everybody that Dorothy was really in charge of the office—I was only a figurehead.

Dorothy and Jack were good friends of Mexican Army General Jesus Jaime Quinones who rode with and then eventually fought against Pancho Villa. The General and his wife, Francis, used to stop and visit at the office on many occasions and Valerie and I were invited to visit their home in Ciudad Acuña. The General was an amazing man—a member of the Mexican Equestrian Team in the 1936 Olympics who rode horses well up to his 84th birthday until he passed away at the age of 86. Jack used to tell stories of bear hunts at the General's ranch in Mexico where the General, after a few tequilas, would put on shooting displays from horseback. Stuff you only now see in movies.

At heart, I have always been a PI, which is the shortened term for an Immigration Patrol Inspector with the U.S. Border Patrol. As a result, I have wondered many times during my career with Customs why in the hell I ever left the Patrol.

In Del Rio, we bought a house on Enchanted Way and found that my neighbor across the back fence was none other than "Cactus Black Jack" Richardson, who was then Deputy Chief of the Del Rio Sector on the Border Patrol. Jack and I became good friends and I cannot say enough about how much he helped me while I was in Del Rio. Jack is gone now but I still miss him.

As previously stated, Mexico has its history and culture founded in Europe and they have their own way of conducting business, which involves "mordida" or the "bite." Simply stated, it is a system where everybody down the line in a business transaction (be it private, commercial, or government) gets a cut. By our standards, it is corruption but it is just their way of doing business.

There is a certain way of dealing with Mexican officials which we had to do to gather intelligence on smuggling activities. Jack and the Border Patrol maintained an outstanding network of intelligence sources in Mexico— unparalleled in my opinion.

Law enforcement officers reading this book can attest that if you want to conduct an investigation in Mexico, you had better know what you are doing and who to deal with or you can land in "the juzgado" (in court) and be in serious trouble. Mexican jails are not pretty and many Mexican officials are involved in crime, by our standards. Technically, investigations in foreign countries must be channeled through the U.S. Department of State and our embassies and consulates abroad, but on the border things are done a little differently for expediency.

Jack and Border Patrol Chief Hugh Williams invited me to join the local Rotary Club and I'm still a member of Rotary International. Doing things for people always gives me a warm feeling in my heart.

I remember Wright's Steakhouse—teaching our daughter, Erin, to dance "The Texas Two-Step" with her stocking feet on my boots, singing with Johnnie and Becky who performed there years ago. The regular crowd in those days included Bit and Joyce Terry. Bit, his given name was Leslie, was a rancher and banker. Joyce was a potter extraordinaire.

I can remember singing with the Bob Grey Band at the Saddle Bronc night club. The band included Pat and Bochie Calderon, who were a son and daughter of Blondie Calderon whose family owned Memo's Restaurant down on San Felipe Creek. Blondie was also the piano player/arranger for Ray Price who would drop in and jam during hunting season and even put on a few free concerts for the people of Del Rio. Steve Terry, son of Bit and Joyce, played an outstanding steel guitar in the Bob Grey Band and was a character.

I recall telling the band that I could sing most any Ray Price song, but only if it's in B-flat because I don't have the range. If the band wasn't certain how to proceed, I'd tell them, "You just play it in B and I'll make it flat."

I remember the Amistad Navy where everybody was an Admiral and you did not have to own a boat to belong. They sponsored boat races on Lake Amistad and I remember Jim Gordon who owned the Saddle Bronc and was a world class boat racer. He was instrumental in bringing boat racing to Del Rio. I also remember George Aubrey's Cripple Creek Saloon, where his wife sat on a swing like in the old west saloon days, was a favorite dining place.

I visited Del Rio about two years ago and was glad to see the Chef's Corner's Restaurant had changed hands. It just was not Del Rio without that law enforcement gathering place.

After Del Rio

We are a law enforcement family.

After Del Rio

In 1985, we transferred to Tucson, Arizona where I finished my career. Justin attended Adams State College in Alamosa, Colorado, played football and is now the Under-Sheriff of Conejos County. We are a law enforcement family. In addition to my son's career and mine, my father was in the military police in World War II and Korea, Valerie's dad was an FBI agent, and our daughter Erin has become a Corrections Officer in Arizona and now lives in Colorado. My wife also worked for the Sheriff's Department in Civil Process in Tucson and I considered her "the Den Mother" down there.

We have now both retired and relocated to the Western Slope of Colorado. My wife keeps me in line because, left to my own devices... well, I didn't get the nickname "Hoot" because I walked the straight and narrow (chuckle).

This book defines me in many ways because I was always trying to find the truth in matters and willing to work together in law enforcement. This book, in essence, is my Epitaph. It is written in memory of Richard and all the law enforcement officers that have paid the ultimate sacrifice. I think there is more personal sacrifice in law enforcement than the public understands. The law enforcement community and system does not work unless agencies cooperate. The only ones that win are the bad guys.

Some people have suggested this book be made into a movie. Considering the escalation of drug trafficking and violence on the border, it might not be a bad idea. The actors, Sam Elliot and someone like Wilfred Brimley, would have to naturally play me (chuckle).

Writing this book had been a healing process for me. It was very hard to investigate the kidnap-murder of my friend, Richard Latham, and I suffered nightmares and recrimination for many years over this matter. Now that this book is finally written and is published, I can finally put "Ol' Richard" in his final rest. Ojala —Spanish translation could be "God grant it." The origin of the word comes from the Spanish Moors and could also mean "I hope, I wish, etc."

Postscript

An unexpected telephone call

Postscript

In September 2020, we were living in Colorado when I received a telephone call from a Houston newspaper reporter who advised me that the shooter, now being referred to as Rafael Calderon-Velasquez, was being released from prison. The reporter asked how I felt about it.

Remembering that the shooter had been sentenced to serve for life, I said, "Well, considering the cold-blooded nature of the crime, I think he should remain in prison for the rest of his life."

Calderon-Velasquez had spent 36 years in a federal prison in Terre Haute, Indiana. He was released into state custody on August 25, and, in September, Texas Rangers traveled to Indiana to bring him back to Maverick County where the original state charges had been filed. As I understand it, the prison authorities could have released the shooter anywhere, but they chose to send him right back to Del Rio International Airport.

I wasn't there, but news reports from that time state that, when the plane landed in Del Rio, a group of border patrol agents as well as other law enforcement officers formed a line and stood silently on the tarmac as the shooter exited the plane.

Later, while watching television, I actually saw the shooter being escorted back to and released in Mexico. Seeing that and still dealing with the reporter's surprise announcement brought back very sad memories.

Not long after these traumatic events, I watched television programs celebrating the work of the Tunnels to Towers Foundation in supporting the families of fallen law enforcement officers and first responders. At the time of Richard Latham's murder, the family received absolutely no assistance from the government.

I was inspired by the work of the Tunnels to Towers Foundation which made me think about ways in which I could help. And that led me to the decision to republish this book and donate all the proceeds to the Foundation.

If you received this book as a gift, please consider making a donation in Richard Latham's name to:

The Tunnel to Towers Foundation
2361 Hylan Blvd.
Staten Island, NY 10306
(718) 987-1931
Website: https://t2t.org/

PROUD
SUPPORTER
OF THE

Tunnel TO **Towers**
Foundation
T2T.ORG

Our Programs

★ The Foundation's *Smart Home Program* builds mortgage-free *smart homes* for our most catastrophically injured veterans and first responders.

★ The *Fallen First Responder Home Program* pays off the mortgages of fallen law enforcement officers and firefighters killed in the line of duty that leave behind young children.

★ The *Gold Star Family Home Program* honors the legacy of those who made the ultimate sacrifice while serving our country. The Foundation will provide a mortgage-free home to surviving spouses with young children.

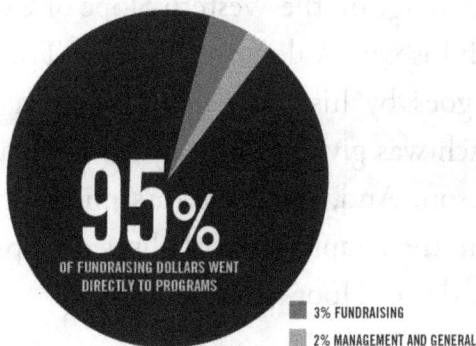

95%
OF FUNDRAISING DOLLARS WENT
DIRECTLY TO PROGRAMS

3% FUNDRAISING
2% MANAGEMENT AND GENERAL

Tunnel to Towers' program service percentage on average is 95%
95 Cents Out of Every Dollar
goes directly to our programs and services.

Tunnel to Towers Foundation is recognized by the IRS as a 501 (c)(3) tax-exempt organization. Our EIN number is 02-0554654. Please consult with your tax advisor regarding the deductibility of your contribution.

About the Author

Dennis Wade Harlan was born in the State of Washington and served a total of 30 years as a federal law enforcement officer. He started his career as an Immigration Patrol Inspector with the U.S. Border Patrol in 1966. In 1970, he became a Special Agent with the U.S. Customs Office of Investigation. He retired in Tucson, Arizona in 1996 and now resides in Cedaredge on the Western Slope of Colorado with his wife, Valerie, of 55 years. These days, he goes by his nickname "Hoot," a handle which was given to him by his compadres in Tucson. And, since Valerie's middle name is Ann, the couple currently lives on a property called the "Hoot-n-Annie Ranch."

Suggested Readings

The Gun That Wasn't There
by Russell Smith

One Ranger and One Ranger Returns
by Joaquin Jackson

O Plata O Plomo?
by James Kuykendall

God's Other Son
by Don Imus

ELEVATION PRESS
OF COLORADO

Your One-Stop Publishing Option

Established 1976

As an independent publisher, we are actively seeking authors who desire to publish their work. For such individuals, we provide design and formatting services. Starting with an author's Microsoft Word document, we produce a book cover and interior pages which the author can submit to a traditional printer or to a print-on-demand service, such as Kindle Direct Publishing (KDP) or IngramSpark. Depending on the complexity of your book, we may also be able to convert the print PDF into a reflowable e-book.

We have successfully formatted a variety of published books including memoirs, children's books, novels, and works of non-fiction.

For more information, visit our website:
elevation-press-books.com

www.ingramcontent.com/pod-product-compliance
Lightning Source LLC
Chambersburg PA
CBHW052033270326
41931CB00012B/2476